FOREWORD

The collection of "Everything Will Be Okay" travel phrasebooks published by T&P Books is designed for people traveling abroad for tourism and business. The phrasebooks contain what matters most - the essentials for basic communication. This is an indispensable set of phrases to "survive" while abroad.

This phrasebook will help you in most cases where you need to ask something, get directions, find out how much something costs, etc. It can also resolve difficult communication situations where gestures just won't help.

This book contains a lot of phrases that have been grouped according to the most relevant topics. You'll also find a mini dictionary with useful words - numbers, time, calendar, colors...

Take "Everything Will Be Okay" phrasebook with you on the road and you'll have an irreplaceable traveling companion who will help you find your way out of any situation and teach you to not fear speaking with foreigners.

TABLE OF CONTENTS

T&P Books Publishing

T&P Books Publishing

PHRASEBOOK

– ARMENIAN –

By Andrey Taranov

THE MOST IMPORTANT PHRASES

This phrasebook contains
the most important
phrases and questions
for basic communication
Everything you need
to survive overseas

T&P BOOKS

Phrasebook + 250-word dictionary

English-Armenian phrasebook & mini dictionary

By Andrey Taranov

The collection of "Everything Will Be Okay" travel phrasebooks published by T&P Books is designed for people traveling abroad for tourism and business. The phrasebooks contain what matters most - the essentials for basic communication. This is an indispensable set of phrases to "survive" while abroad.

You'll also find a mini dictionary with 250 useful words required for everyday communication - the names of months and days of the week, measurements, family members, and more.

T&P Books Publishing
www.tpbooks.com

ISBN: 978-1-78492-422-5

This book is also available in E-book formats.
Please visit www.tpbooks.com or the major online bookstores.

PRONUNCIATION

Letter	Armenian example	T&P phonetic alphabet	English example

Vowels

Letter	Armenian example	T&P phonetic alphabet	English example
ա	սազ	[ɑ]	shorter than in park, card
ե [1]	ելակ	[e]	elm, medal
ե [2]	մեխակ	[ɛ]	man, bad
է	էժան	[ɛ]	man, bad
ի	միս	[i]	shorter than in feet
ո [3]	ոզնի	[vɔ]	divorce, to avoid
ո [4]	բողորել	[o]	pod, John
ու	թոչուն	[u]	book
օ [5]	օգտվել	[o]	pod, John
ը	ընտրել	[ə]	driver, teacher

Consonants

Letter	Armenian example	T&P phonetic alphabet	English example
բ	բարձր	[b]	baby, book
գ	գագաթ	[g]	game, gold
դ	դերասան	[d]	day, doctor
զ	զվարճանալ	[z]	zebra, please
թ	թեն	[th]	don't have
ժ	ժամանցույց	[ʒ]	forge, pleasure
լ	լվացվել	[l]	lace, people
խ	ախտորոշում	[h], [x]	as in Scots loch
ծ	ծիածան	[ts]	cats, tsetse fly
կ	փակել	[k]	clock, kiss
հ	հիհարել	[h]	home, have
ձ	ձատրաձող	[dz]	beads, kids
ղ	մեղր	[ɣ]	between [g] and [h]
ճ	ճանիճ	[tʃ]	church, French
մ	ամայի	[m]	magic, milk
յ	նայել	[j]	yes, New York
ն	կանգառ	[n]	name, normal
շ	շուն	[ʃ]	machine, shark
չ	կրակայրիչ	[tʃh]	hitchhiker
պ	ամպ	[p]	pencil, private

Letter	Armenian example	T&P phonetic alphabet	English example
Ջ	ջիջել	[dʒ]	joke, general
Ռ	ռառ	[r]	rice, radio
Ս	մաս	[s]	city, boss
Վ	ավել	[v]	very, river
Տ	պատուհան	[t]	tourist, trip
Ր	կարել	[r]	soft [r]
Ց	բաց	[tsh]	let's handle it
Փ	սարսափ	[ph]	top hat
Ք	դեմք	[k]	clock, kiss
Ֆ	ասֆալտ	[f]	face, food

Comments

[1] at the beginning of a word
[2] in the middle
[3] at the beginning of a word
[4] in the middle
[5] at the beginning of a word usually

LIST OF ABBREVIATIONS

English abbreviations

ab.	-	about
adj	-	adjective
adv	-	adverb
anim.	-	animate
as adj	-	attributive noun used as adjective
e.g.	-	for example
etc.	-	et cetera
fam.	-	familiar
fem.	-	feminine
form.	-	formal
inanim.	-	inanimate
masc.	-	masculine
math	-	mathematics
mil.	-	military
n	-	noun
pl	-	plural
pron.	-	pronoun
sb	-	somebody
sing.	-	singular
sth	-	something
v aux	-	auxiliary verb
vi	-	intransitive verb
vi, vt	-	intransitive, transitive verb
vt	-	transitive verb

Armenian punctuation

՛	-	Exclamation mark
՞	-	Question mark
,	-	Comma

ARMENIAN
PHRASEBOOK

This section contains
important phrases that may
come in handy in various
real-life situations.
The phrasebook will help
you ask for directions, clarify
a price, buy tickets, and
order food at a restaurant

T&P Books Publishing

PHRASEBOOK CONTENTS

T&P Books Publishing

Excuse me, ...	Ներեցեք, ... [nerets'eq, ...]
Hello.	Բարև Ձեզ: [bar'ev dzez]
Thank you.	Շնորհակալություն: [shnorhakaluty'un]
Good bye.	Ցտեսություն: [tstesuty'un]
Yes.	Այո: [ay'o]
No.	Ոչ: [voch]
I don't know.	Ես չգիտեմ: [yes chgit'em]
Where? | Where to? | When?	Ո՞րտեղ: Ո՞ւր: Ե՞րբ: [vort'egh? ur? yerb?]

I need ...	Ինձ հարկավոր է ... [indz harkav'or e ...]
I want ...	Ես ուզում եմ ... [yes uz'um em ...]
Do you have ...?	Դուք ունե՞ք ...: [duq un'eq ...?]
Is there a ... here?	Այստեղ կա՞ ...: [ayst'egh ka ...?]
May I ...?	Ես կարո՞ղ եմ ...: [yes kar'ogh em ...?]
..., please (polite request)	Խնդրում եմ [khndrum em]

I'm looking for ...	Ես փնտրում եմ ... [yes pntrum am ...]
restroom	զուգարան [zugar'an]
ATM	բանկոմատ [bankom'at]
pharmacy (drugstore)	դեղատուն [deghat'un]
hospital	հիվանդանոց [hivandan'ots]
police station	ոստիկանության բաժանմունք [vostikanuty'an bazhanm'unq]
subway	մետրո [metr'o]

taxi	տաքսի [tax'i]
train station	կայարան [kayar'an]

My name is ...	Իմ անունը ... է: [im an'uny ... e]
What's your name?	Ձեր անունն ի՞նչ է: [dzer an'unn inch e?]
Could you please help me?	Օգնեցեք ինձ, խնդրեմ: [ognets'eq indz, khndrem]
I've got a problem.	Ես խնդիր ունեմ: [yes khndir un'em]
I don't feel well.	Ես ինձ վատ եմ զգում: [yes indz vat am zgum]
Call an ambulance!	Շտապ օգնություն կանչեք: [shtap ognuty'un kanch'eq!]
May I make a call?	Կարո՞ղ եմ զանգահարել: [kar'ogh am zangahar'el?]

I'm sorry.	Ներեցեք [nerets'eq]
You're welcome.	Խնդրեմ [kndrem]

I, me	Ես [yes]
you (inform.)	դու [du]
he	նա [na]
she	նա [na]
they (masc.)	նրանք [nrank]
they (fem.)	նրանք [nrank]
we	մենք [menq]
you (pl)	դուք [duq]
you (sg, form.)	Դուք [duq]

ENTRANCE	ՄՈՒՏՔ [mutq]
EXIT	ԵԼՔ [yelq]
OUT OF ORDER	ՉԻ ԱՇԽԱՏՈՒՄ [chi ashkhat'um]
CLOSED	ՓԱԿ Է [pak e]

OPEN	ԲԱՑ Է
	[bats e]
FOR WOMEN	ԿԱՆԱՆՑ ՀԱՄԱՐ
	[kan'ants ham'ar]
FOR MEN	ՏՂԱՄԱՐԴԿԱՆՑ ՀԱՄԱՐ
	[tghamardk'ants ham'ar]

Questions

Where?
Որտե՞ղ:
[vort'egh?]

Where to?
Ո՞ւր:
[ur?]

Where from?
Որտեղի՞ց:
[vortegh'its?]

Why?
Ինչո՞ւ:
[inch'u?]

For what reason?
Ինչի՞ համար:
[inch'i ham'ar?]

When?
Ե՞րբ:
[yerb?]

How long?
Ինչքա՞ն ժամանակ:
[inchq'an zhaman'ak?]

At what time?
Ժամը քանիսի՞ն:
[zh'amy qanis'in?]

How much?
Ի՞նչ արժե:
[inch arzh'e?]

Do you have ...?
Դուք ունե՞ք ...:
[duq un'eq ...?]

Where is ...?
Որտե՞ղ է գտնվում ...:
[vort'egh e gtnvum ...?]

What time is it?
Ժամը քանի՞սն է:
[zh'amy qan'isn e?]

May I make a call?
Կարո՞ղ եմ զանգահարել:
[kar'ogh am zangahar'el?]

Who's there?
Ո՞վ է:
[ov e?]

Can I smoke here?
Կարո՞ղ եմ այստեղ ծխել:
[kar'ogh am ayst'egh tskhel?]

May I ...?
Ես կարո՞ղ եմ ...:
[yes kar'ogh em ...?]

Needs

I'd like ...	Ես կուզենայի ... [yes kuzen'ayi ...]
I don't want ...	Ես չեմ ուզում ... [yes chem uz'um ...]
I'm thirsty.	Ես ծարավ եմ: [yes tsar'av am]
I want to sleep.	Ես ուզում եմ քնել: [yes uz'um am qnel]

I want ...	Ես ուզում եմ ... [yes uz'um am ...]
to wash up	լվացվել [lvatsv'el]
to brush my teeth	ատամներս մաքրել [atamn'ers maqr'el]
to rest a while	մի քիչ հանգստանալ [mi qich hangstan'al]
to change my clothes	շորերս փոխել [shor'ers pokh'el]

to go back to the hotel	վերադառնալ հյուրանոց [veradarn'al hyuran'ots]
to buy ...	գնել ... [gnel ...]
to go to ...	գնալ ... [gnal ...]
to visit ...	այցելել ... [aytsel'el ...]
to meet with ...	հանդիպել ... հետ [handip'el ... het]
to make a call	զանգահարել [zangahar'el]

I'm tired.	Ես հոգնել եմ: [yes hogn'el am]
We are tired.	Մենք հոգնել ենք: [menq hogn'el enq]
I'm cold.	Ես մրսում եմ: [yes mrsum am]
I'm hot.	Ես շոգում եմ: [yes shog'um am]
I'm OK.	Ես լավ եմ: [yes lav am]

I need to make a call.

Ես պետք է զանգահարեմ:
[yes petq e zangahar'em]

I need to go to the restroom.

Ես զուգարան եմ ուզում:
[yes zugar'an am uz'um]

I have to go.

Գնալուս ժամանակն է:
[gnal'us zhaman'akn e]

I have to go now.

Ես պետք է գնամ:
[yes petq e gnam]

Asking for directions

Excuse me, ...
Ներեցեք, ...
[nerets'eq, ...]

Where is ...?
Որտե՞ղ է գտնվում ...
[vort'egh e gtnvum ...?]

Which way is ...?
Ո՞ր ուղղությամբ է գտնվում ...
[vor ughghuty'amb e gtnv'um ...?]

Could you help me, please?
Օգնեցեք ինձ, խնդրեմ:
[ognets'eq indz, khndrem]

I'm looking for ...
Ես փնտրում եմ ...
[yes pntrum am ...]

I'm looking for the exit.
Ես փնտրում եմ ելքը:
[yes pntrum am y'elky]

I'm going to ...
Ես գնում եմ ...
[yes gnum am ...]

Am I going the right way to ...?
Ես ճի՞շտ եմ գնում ...:
[yes chisht am gnum ...?]

Is it far?
Դա հեռու՞ է:
[da her'u e?]

Can I get there on foot?
Ես կհասնե՞մ այնտեղ ոտքով:
[yes khasn'em aynt'egh votq'ov?]

Can you show me on the map?
Ցույց տվեք ինձ քարտեզի վրա, խնդրում եմ:
[tsuyts tveq indz qartez'i vra, khndrum am]

Show me where we are right now.
Ցույց տվեք՝ որտեղ ենք մենք հիմա:
[tsuyts tveq vort'egh enk menq him'a]

Here
Այստեղ
[ayst'egh]

There
Այնտեղ
[aynt'egh]

This way
Այստեղ
[ayst'egh]

Turn right.
Թեքվեք աջ:
[tekv'ek aj]

Turn left.
Թեքվեք ձախ:
[tekv'ek dzakh]

first (second, third) turn
առաջին (երկրորդ, երրորդ) շրջադարձ
[araj'in (yerkr'ord, err'ord) shrjad'ardz]

to the right
դեպի աջ
[dep'i aj]

to the left

դեպի ձախ
[dep'i dzakh]

Go straight.

Գնացեք ուղիղ:
[gnats'ek ugh'igh]

Signs

WELCOME!	ԲԱՐԻ՜ ԳԱԼՈՒՍՏ: [bar'i gal'ust!]
ENTRANCE	ՄՈՒՏՔ [mutq]
EXIT	ԵԼՔ [yelq]

PUSH	ԴԵՊԻ ՆԵՐՍ [dep'i ners]
PULL	ԴԵՊԻ ԴՈՒՐՍ [dep'i durs]
OPEN	ԲԱՑ Է [bats e]
CLOSED	ՓԱԿ Է [pak e]

FOR WOMEN	ԿԱՆԱՆՑ ՀԱՄԱՐ [kan'ants ham'ar]
FOR MEN	ՏՂԱՄԱՐԴԿԱՆՑ ՀԱՄԱՐ [tghamardk'ants ham'ar]
MEN, GENTS	ՏՂԱՄԱՐԴԿԱՆՑ ԶՈՒԳԱՐԱՆ [tghamardk'ants zugar'an]
WOMEN, LADIES	ԿԱՆԱՆՑ ԶՈՒԳԱՐԱՆ [kan'ants zugar'an]

DISCOUNTS	ԶԵՂՉ [zeghch]
SALE	ԻՍՊԱՌ ՎԱՃԱՌՔ [isp'ar vach'ark]
FREE	ԱՆՎՃԱՐ [anvch'ar]
NEW!	ՆՈՐՈ՛ՒՅԹ [nor'uyt]
ATTENTION!	ՈՒՇԱԴՐՈՒԹՅՈ՛ՒՆ [ushadruty'un]

NO VACANCIES	ԱԶԱՏ ՀԱՄԱՐՆԵՐ ՉԿԱՆ [az'at hamarn'er chk'an]
RESERVED	ՊԱՏՎԻՐՎԱԾ Է [patvirv'ats e]
ADMINISTRATION	ԱԴՄԻՆԻՍՏՐԱՑԻԱ [administratsi'a]
STAFF ONLY	ՄԻԱՅՆ ԱՆՁՆԱԿԱԶՄԻ ՀԱՄԱՐ [mi'ayn andznakazm'i ham'ar]

BEWARE OF THE DOG!	ԿԱՏԱՂԱԾ ՇՈւՆ [katagh'ats shun]
NO SMOKING!	ՉԾԽԵԼ [chtskh'el]
DO NOT TOUCH!	ՁԵՌՔԵՐՈՎ ՉԴԻՊՉԵԼ [dzerkyer'ov chdipch'el]
DANGEROUS	ՎՏԱՆԳԱՎՈՐ Է [vtangav'or e]
DANGER	ՎՏԱՆԳ [vtang]
HIGH VOLTAGE	ԲԱՐՁՐ ԼԱՐՈւՄ [bardzr lar'um]
NO SWIMMING!	ԼՈՂԱԼՆ ԱՐԳԵԼՎՈւՄ Է [logh'aln argelv'um e]

OUT OF ORDER	ՉԻ ԱՇԽԱՏՈւՄ [chi ashkhat'um]
FLAMMABLE	ԴՅՈւՐԱՎԱՌ Է [dyurav'ar e]
FORBIDDEN	ԱՐԳԵԼՎԱԾ Է [argelv'ats e]
NO TRESPASSING!	ՄՈւՏՔՆ ԱՐԳԵԼՎԱԾ Է [mutkn argelv'ats e]
WET PAINT	ՆԵՐԿՎԱԾ Է [nerkv'ats e]

CLOSED FOR RENOVATIONS	ՓԱԿՎԱԾ Է ՎԵՐԱՆՈՐՈԳՄԱՆ [pakv'ats e veranorogm'an]
WORKS AHEAD	ՎԵՐԱՆՈՐՈԳՄԱՆ ԱՇԽԱՏԱՆՔՆԵՐ [veranorogm'an ashkhatankn'er]
DETOUR	ՇՐՋԱՆՑՈւՄ [shrjants'um]

Transportation. General phrases

plane	ինքնաթիռ [inqnat'ir]
train	գնացք [gnatsq]
bus	ավտոբուս [avtob'us]
ferry	լաստանավ [lastanav]
taxi	տաքսի [tax'i]
car	ավտոմեքենա [avtomeqen'a]
schedule	չվացուցակ [chvatsuts'ak]
Where can I see the schedule?	Որտե՞ղ կարելի է նայել չվացուցակը: [vort'egh karel'i e nay'el chvatsuts'aky?]
workdays (weekdays)	աշխատանքային օրեր [ashkhatankay'in or'er]
weekends	հանգստյան օրեր [hangsty'an or'er]
holidays	տոնական օրեր [tonak'an or'er]
DEPARTURE	ՄԵԿՆՈՒՄ [mekn'um]
ARRIVAL	ԺԱՄԱՆՈՒՄ [zhaman'um]
DELAYED	ՈՒՇԱՑՈՒՄ [ushats'um]
CANCELED	ՉԵՂՅԱԼ [cheghy'al]
next (train, etc.)	հաջորդ [haj'ord]
first	առաջին [araj'in]
last	վերջին [verj'in]
When is the next ...?	Ե՞րբ է լինելու հաջորդ ...: [yerb e linel'u haj'ordy ...?]
When is the first ...?	Ե՞րբ է մեկնում առաջին ...: [yerb e mekn'um araj'in ...?]

When is the last ...?

Ե՞րբ է մեկնում վերջին ...:
[yerb e mekn'um verj'in ...?]

transfer (change of trains, etc.)

նստափոխ
[nstap'okh]

to make a transfer

նստափոխ կատարել
[nstap'okh katar'el]

Do I need to make a transfer?

Ես պետք է նստափո՞խ կատարեմ:
[yes petq e nstap'okh katar'em?]

Buying tickets

Where can I buy tickets?	Որտե՞ղ կարող եմ տոմսեր գնել: [vort'egh kar'ogh am toms'er gnel?]
ticket	տոմս [toms]
to buy a ticket	տոմս գնել [toms gnel]
ticket price	տոմսի արժեքը [t'omsi arzh'eqy]

Where to?	Ո՞ւր: [ur?]
To what station?	Մինչև ո՞ր կայարան: [minch'ev vor kayar'an?]
I need ...	Ինձ հարկավոր է ... [indz harkav'or e ...]
one ticket	մեկ տոմս [mek toms]
two tickets	երկու տոմս [yerk'u toms]
three tickets	երեք տոմս [yer'ek toms]

one-way	մեկ ուղղությամբ [mek ughghuty'amb]
round-trip	վերադարձով [veradardz'ov]
first class	առաջին դաս [araj'in das]
second class	երկրորդ դաս [yerkr'ord das]

today	այսօր [ays'or]
tomorrow	վաղը [v'aghy]
the day after tomorrow	վաղը չէ մյուս օրը [v'aghy che my'us 'ory]
in the morning	առավոտյան [aravoty'an]
in the afternoon	ցերեկը [tser'eky]
in the evening	երեկոյան [yerekoy'an]

aisle seat

տեղ միջանցքի մոտ
[tegh mijantsk'i mot]

window seat

տեղ պատուհանի մոտ
[tegh patuhan'i mot]

How much?

Ինչքա՞ն:
[inchq'an?]

Can I pay by credit card?

Կարո՞ղ եմ վճարել քարտով:
[kar'ogh am vchar'el qart'ov?]

Bus

bus	ավտոբուս [avtob'us]
intercity bus	միջքաղաքային ավտոբուս [mijqaghaqay'in avtob'us]
bus stop	ավտոբուսի կանգար [avtob'usi kang'ar]
Where's the nearest bus stop?	Որտե՞ղ է մոտակա ավտոբուսի կանգառը: [vort'egh e motak'a avtob'usi kang'ary?]
number (bus ~, etc.)	համար [ham'ar]
Which bus do I take to get to …?	Ո՞ր ավտոբուսն է գնում մինչև …: [vor avtob'usn e gnum minch'ev …?]
Does this bus go to …?	Այս ավտոբուսը գնո՞ւմ է մինչև …: [ays avtob'usy gnum e minch'ev …?]
How frequent are the buses?	Որքա՞ն հաճախ են երթևեկում ավտոբուսները: [vorq'an hach'akh en gnum avtob'usnery?]
every 15 minutes	յուրաքանչյուր տասնհինգ րոպեն մեկ [yurakanchy'ur tasnh'ing rop'en mek]
every half hour	յուրաքանչյուր կեսժամը մեկ [yurakanchy'ur kes jam'y mek]
every hour	յուրաքանչյուր ժամը մեկ [yurakanchy'ur jam'y mek]
several times a day	օրեկան մի քանի անգամ [orek'an mi qan'i ang'am]
… times a day	օրեկան … անգամ [orek'an … ang'am]
schedule	չվացուցակ [chvatsuts'ak]
Where can I see the schedule?	Որտե՞ղ կարելի է նայել չվացուցակը: [vort'egh karel'i e nay'el chvatsuts'aky?]
When is the next bus?	Ե՞րբ է լինելու հաջորդ ավտոբուսը: [yerb e linel'u haj'ord avtob'usy?]
When is the first bus?	Ե՞րբ է մեկնում առաջին ավտոբուսը: [yerb e mekn'um araj'in avtob'usy?]
When is the last bus?	Ե՞րբ է մեկնում վերջին ավտոբուսը: [yerb e mekn'um verj'in avtob'usy?]

stop

կանգառ
[kang'ar]

next stop

հաջորդ կանգառ
[haj'ord kang'ar]

last stop (terminus)

վերջին կանգառ
[verj'in kang'ar]

Stop here, please.

Կանգնեք այստեղ, խնդրում եմ:
[kangn'ek ayst'egh, khndrum em]

Excuse me, this is my stop.

Թույլ տվեք, սա իմ կանգառն է:
[tuyl tveq, sa im kang'arn e]

Train

train	գնացք
	[gnatsq]
suburban train	մերձքաղաքային գնացք
	[merdzqaghaqay'in gnatsq]
long-distance train	հեռագնաց գնացք
	[heragn'ac gnatsq]
train station	կայարան
	[kayar'an]
Excuse me, where is the exit to the platform?	Ներեցեք, որտե՞ղ է ելքը դեպի գնացքները:
	[nerets'eq, vort'egh e y'elky dep'i gnatsqn'ery?]

Does this train go to ...?	Այս գնացքը գնո՞ւմ է մինչև ...:
	[ays gn'atsqy gnum e minch'ev ...?]
next train	հաջորդ գնացքը
	[haj'ord gn'atsqy]
When is the next train?	Ե՞րբ է լինելու հաջորդ գնացքը:
	[yerb e linel'u haj'ord gn'atsqy?]
Where can I see the schedule?	Որտե՞ղ կարելի է տեսնել չվացուցակը:
	[vort'egh karel'i e nay'el chvatsuts'aky?]
From which platform?	Ո՞ր հարթակից:
	[vor hartak'its?]
When does the train arrive in ...?	Ե՞րբ է գնացքը ժամանում ...:
	[yerb e gn'atsqy zhaman'um ...?]

Please help me.	Օգնեցեք ինձ, խնդրեմ:
	[ognets'eq indz, khndrem]
I'm looking for my seat.	Ես փնտրում եմ իմ տեղը:
	[yes pntrum am im t'eghy]
We're looking for our seats.	Մենք փնտրում ենք մեր տեղերը:
	[menq pntrum enq mer tegh'ery]

My seat is taken.	Իմ տեղը զբաղված է:
	[im t'eghy zbaghv'ats e]
Our seats are taken.	Մեր տեղերը զբաղված են:
	[mer tegh'ery zbaghv'ats en]
I'm sorry but this is my seat.	Ներեցեք, խնդրում եմ, բայց սա իմ տեղն է:
	[nerets'eq, khndrum am, bayts sa im t'eghn e]

Is this seat taken?

Այս տեղն զզւ՞տ է:
[ays teghn az'at e?]

May I sit here?

Կարո՞ղ եմ այստեղ նստել:
[kar'ogh am ayst'egh nstel?]

On the train. Dialogue (No ticket)

Ticket, please.
Ձեր տոմսը, խնդրեմ:
[dzer t'omsy, khndrem]

I don't have a ticket.
Ես տոմս չունեմ:
[yes toms chun'em]

I lost my ticket.
Ես կորցրել եմ իմ տոմսը:
[yes kortsr'el am im t'omsy]

I forgot my ticket at home.
Ես մոռացել եմ իմ տոմսը տանը:
[yes morats'el am im t'omsy t'any]

You can buy a ticket from me.
Դուք կարող եք գնել տոմս ինձանից:
[indzan'its]

You will also have to pay a fine.
Նաև դուք պետք է վճարեք տուգանեք:
[na'ev duq petq e vchar'eq tug'ank]

Okay.
Լավ:
[lav]

Where are you going?
Ո՞ւր եք մեկնում:
[ur eq mekn'um?]

I'm going to ...
Ես գնում եմ մինչև ...
[yes gnum am minch'ev ...]

How much? I don't understand.
Ինչքա՞ն: Ես չեմ հասկանում:
[inchq'an? yes chem haskan'um]

Write it down, please.
Գրեք, խնդրում եմ:
[grek, khndrum em]

Okay. Can I pay with a credit card?
Լավ: Կարո՞ղ եմ վճարել քարտով:
[lav kar'ogh am vchar'el qart'ov?]

Yes, you can.
Այո, կարող եք:
[ay'o, kar'ogh eq]

Here's your receipt.
Ահա ձեր անդորրագիրը:
[ah'a dzer andorag'iry]

Sorry about the fine.
Ցավում եմ տուգանքի համար:
[tsav'um am tugank'i ham'ar]

That's okay. It was my fault.
Ոչինչ: Դա իմ մեղքն է:
[voch'inch. da im meghqn e]

Enjoy your trip.
Հաճելի ճանապարհորդություն:
[hachel'i chanaparhoduty'un]

Taxi

taxi	տաքսի [tax'i]
taxi driver	տաքսու վարորդ [tax'u var'ord]
to catch a taxi	տաքսի բռնել [tax'i brnel]
taxi stand	տաքսու կանգառ [tax'u kang'ar]
Where can I get a taxi?	Որտե՞ղ կարող եմ տաքսի վերցնել: [vort'egh kar'ogh am tax'i vertsn'el?]
to call a taxi	տաքսի կանչել [tax'i kanch'el]
I need a taxi.	Ինձ տաքսի է հարկավոր: [indz tax'i e harkav'or]
Right now.	Հենց հիմա: [hents him'a]
What is your address (location)?	Ձեր հասցե՞ն: [dzer hasc'en?]
My address is ...	Իմ հասցեն ... [im hasc'en ...]
Your destination?	Ո՞ւր եք գնալու: [ur eq gnal'u?]
Excuse me, ...	Ներեցեք, ... [nerets'eq, ...]
Are you available?	Ազա՞տ եք: [az'at eq?]
How much is it to get to ...?	Ի՞նչ արժե հասնել մինչև ...: [inch arzh'e hasn'el minch'ev ...?]
Do you know where it is?	Դուք գիտե՞ք որտեղ է դա: [duq git'eq vort'egh e da?]
Airport, please.	Օդանավակայան, խնդրում եմ: [odanavakay'an, khndrum em]
Stop here, please.	Կանգնեցրեք այստեղ, խնդրում եմ: [kangnetsr'eq ayst'egh, khndrum em]
It's not here.	Դա այստեղ չէ: [da ayst'egh che]
This is the wrong address.	Դա սխալ հասցե է: [da skhal hasc'e e]
Turn left.	դեպի ձախ [dep'i dzakh]
Turn right.	դեպի աջ [dep'i aj]

How much do I owe you?	Որքա՞ն պետք է վճարեմ:
	[vorq'an petq e vchar'em?]
I'd like a receipt, please.	Տվեք ինձ չեքը, խնդրում եմ:
	[tveq indz ch'eqy, khndrum em]
Keep the change.	Մանրը պետք չէ:
	[m'anry petq che]

Would you please wait for me?	Սպասեք ինձ, խնդրում եմ:
	[spas'eq indz, khndrum em]
five minutes	հինգ րոպե
	[hing rop'e]
ten minutes	տաս րոպե
	[tas rop'e]
fifteen minutes	տասնհինգ րոպե
	[tasnh'ing rop'e]
twenty minutes	քսան րոպե
	[qsan rop'e]
half an hour	կես ժամ
	[kes zham]

Hotel

Hello.	Բարև Ձեզ:
	[bar'ev dzez]
My name is ...	Իմ անունը ... է:
	[im an'uny ... e]
I have a reservation.	Ես համար եմ ամրագրել:
	[yes ham'ar am amragr'el]

I need ...	Ինձ հարկավոր է ...
	[indz harkav'or e ...]
a single room	մեկտեղանոց համար
	[mekteghan'ots ham'ar]
a double room	երկտեղանոց համար
	[yerkteghan'ots ham'ar]
How much is that?	Որքա՞ն այն արժե:
	[vorq'an ayn arzh'e?]
That's a bit expensive.	Դա մի քիչ թանկ է:
	[da mi qich tank e]

Do you have any other options?	Ունե՞ք որևէ այլ տարբերակ:
	[un'eq vorev'e 'ayl tarber'ak?]
I'll take it.	Ես դա կվերցնեմ:
	[yes da kvertsn'em]
I'll pay in cash.	Ես կանխիկ կվճարեմ:
	[yes kankh'ik kvchar'em]

I've got a problem.	Ես խնդիր ունեմ:
	[yes khnd'ir un'em]
My ... is broken.	Իմ ... փչացել է:
	[im ... pchats'el e]
My ... is out of order.	Իմ ... չի աշխատում:
	[im ... chi ashkhat'um]
TV	հեռուստացույցը
	[herustats'uytsy]
air conditioning	օդորակիչը
	[odorak'ichy]
tap	ծորակը
	[tsor'aky]

shower	ցնցուղը
	[tsnts'ughy]
sink	լվացարանը
	[lvatsar'any]
safe	չհրկիզվող պահարանը
	[chhrkizv'ogh pahar'any]

door lock	կողպեքը [koghp'eqy]
electrical outlet	վարդակը [vard'aky]
hairdryer	ֆենը [f'eny]

I don't have ...	Ես ... չունեմ: [yes ... chun'em]
water	ջուր [jur]
light	լույս [luys]
electricity	հոսանք [hos'anq]

Can you give me ...?	Կարո՞ղ եք ինձ տալ ...: [kar'ogh eq indz tal ...?]
a towel	սրբիչ [srbich]
a blanket	ծածկոց [tsatsk'ots]
slippers	հողաթափեր [hoghatap'er]
a robe	խալաթ [khal'at]
shampoo	շամպուն [shamp'un]
soap	օճառ [och'ar]

I'd like to change rooms.	Ես կցանկանայի փոխել համարս: [yes ktsankan'ayi pokh'el ham'ars]
I can't find my key.	Ես չեմ կարողանում գտնել իմ բանալին: [yes chem karoghan'um gtnel im banal'in]
Could you open my room, please?	Խնդրում եմ, բացեք իմ համարը: [khndrum em, bats'ek im ham'ary]
Who's there?	Ո՞վ է: [ov e?]
Come in!	Մտեք: [mteq!]
Just a minute!	Մեկ րոպե: [mek rope!]
Not right now, please.	Խնդրում եմ, հիմա չէ: [khndrum em, him'a che]

Come to my room, please.	Խնդրում եմ, ինձ մոտ մտեք: [khndrum em, indz mot mteq]
I'd like to order food service.	Ես ուզում եմ ունտելիք համար պատվիրել: [yes uz'um am utel'iq ham'ar patvir'el]

My room number is …

Իմ սենյակի համարը … է։
[im senyak'i ham'ary … e]

I'm leaving …

Ես մեկնում եմ …
[yes mekn'um am …]

We're leaving …

Մենք մեկնում ենք …
[menq mekn'um enq …]

right now

հիմա
[him'a]

this afternoon

այսօր ճաշից հետո
[ays'or chash'its het'o]

tonight

այսօր երեկոյան
[ays'or yerekoy'an]

tomorrow

վաղը
[v'aghy]

tomorrow morning

վաղն առավոտյան
[v'aghn aravoty'an]

tomorrow evening

վաղը երեկոյան
[v'aghy yerekoy'an]

the day after tomorrow

վաղը չէ մյուս օրը
[v'aghy che my'us 'ory]

I'd like to pay.

Ես կուզենայի հաշիվը վճարել։
[yes kuzen'ayi hash'ivy pak'el]

Everything was wonderful.

Ամեն ինչ հոյակապ էր։
[am'en inch hoyak'ap er]

Where can I get a taxi?

Որտե՞ղ կարող եմ տաքսի վերցնել։
[vort'egh kar'ogh am tax'i vertsn'el?]

Would you call a taxi for me, please?

Ինձ համար տաքսի կանչեք,
խնդրում եմ։
[indz ham'ar tax'i kanch'eq,
khndrum em]

Restaurant

Can I look at the menu, please?
Կարո՞ղ եմ նայել ձեր ճաշացանկը:
[kar'ogh am nay'el dzer chashats'anky?]

Table for one.
Սեղան մեկ հոգու համար:
[segh'an mek hog'u ham'ar]

There are two (three, four) of us.
Մենք երկուսով (երեքով, չորսով) ենք:
[menq yerkus'ov (yerek'ov, chors'ov) enq]

Smoking
Ծխողների համար
[tskhoghner'i ham'ar]

No smoking
Չծխողների համար
[chtskhoghner'i ham'ar]

Excuse me! (addressing a waiter)
Մոտեցեք խնդրեմ:
[motets'eq khndrem!]

menu
Ճաշացանկ
[chashats'ank]

wine list
Գինեքարտ
[gineq'art]

The menu, please.
Ճաշացանկը, խնդրեմ:
[chashats'anky, khndrem]

Are you ready to order?
Պատրա՞ստ եք պատվիրել:
[patr'ast eq patvir'el?]

What will you have?
Ի՞նչ եք պատվիրելու:
[inch eq patvirel'u?]

I'll have ...
Ես կվերցնեմ ...
[yes kvertsn'em ...]

I'm a vegetarian.
Ես բուսակեր եմ:
[yes busak'er am]

meat
միս
[mis]

fish
ձուկ
[dzuk]

vegetables
բանջարեղեն
[banjaregh'en]

Do you have vegetarian dishes?
Դուք ունե՞ք բուսակերական ճաշատեսակներ:
[duq un'eq busakerak'an chashatesakn'er?]

I don't eat pork.
Ես խոզի միս չեմ ուտում:
[yes kh'ozi mis chem ut'um]

He /she/ doesn't eat meat.
Նա միս չի ուտում:
[na mis chi ut'um]

I am allergic to ...

Ես ...ից ալերգիա ունեմ:
[yes ...its alerg'ia un'em]

Would you please bring me ...

Խնդրում եմ, ինձ ... բերեք:
[khndrum em, indz ... ber'eq]

salt | pepper | sugar

աղ | պղպեղ | շաքար
[agh | pghpegh | shaq'ar]

coffee | tea | dessert

սուրճ | թեյ | աղանդեր
[surch | tey | aghand'er]

water | sparkling | plain

ջուր | գազավորված | չգազավորված
[jur | gazavorv'ats | chgazavorv'ats]

a spoon | fork | knife

գդալ | պատառաքաղ | դանակ
[gdal | pataraq'agh | dan'ak]

a plate | napkin

ափսե | անձեռոցիկ
[aps'e | andzerots'ik]

Enjoy your meal!

Բարի ախորժմա՛կ:
[bar'i akhorzh'ak!]

One more, please.

Էլի բերեք, խնդրում եմ:
[el'i ber'eq, khndrum em]

It was very delicious.

Շատ համեղ էր:
[shat ham'egh er]

check | change | tip

հաշիվ | մանրադրամ | թեյավճար
[hash'iv | manradr'am | tyeyavch'ar]

Check, please.
(Could I have the check, please?)

Հաշիվը, խնդրում եմ:
[hash'ivy, khndrum em]

Can I pay by credit card?

Կարո՞ղ եմ վճարել քարտով:
[kar'ogh am vchar'el qart'ov?]

I'm sorry, there's a mistake here.

Ներեցեք, այստեղ սխալ կա:
[nerets'eq, ayst'egh skhal ka]

Shopping

Can I help you?

Կարո՞ղ եմ օգնել ձեզ։
[kar'ogh am ogn'el dzez?]

Do you have ...?

Դուք ունե՞ք ...:
[duq un'eq ...?]

I'm looking for ...

Ես փնտրում եմ ...
[yes pntrum am ...]

I need ...

Ինձ պետք է ...
[indz petq e ...]

I'm just looking.

Ես ուղղակի նայում եմ:
[yes ughghak'i nay'um am]

We're just looking.

Մենք ուղղակի նայում ենք:
[menq ughgh'aki nay'um enq]

I'll come back later.

Ես ավելի ուշ կայցելեմ:
[yes avel'i ush kaytsel'em]

We'll come back later.

Մենք ավելի ուշ կայցելենք:
[menq avel'i ush kaytsel'enq]

discounts | sale

զեղչեր | իսպառ վաճառք
[zeghch'er | isp'ar vach'arq]

Would you please show me ...

Ցույց տվեք ինձ, խնդրում եմ ...
[tsuyts tveq indz, khndrum em ...]

Would you please give me ...

Տվեք ինձ, խնդրում եմ ...
[tveq indz, khndrum em ...]

Can I try it on?

Կարո՞ղ եմ ես սա փորձել:
[kar'ogh am yes sa pordz'el?]

Excuse me, where's the fitting room?

Ներեցեք, որտե՞ղ է հանդերձարանը:
[nerets'eq, vort'egh e handerdzar'any?]

Which color would you like?

Ի՞նչ գույն եք ուզում:
[inch guyn eq uz'um?]

size | length

չափս | հասակ
[chaps | hasak]

How does it fit?

Եղա՞վ:
[yegh'av?]

How much is it?

Սա ինչքա՞ն արժե:
[sa inchq'an arzh'e?]

That's too expensive.

Դա չափազանց թանկ է:
[da chapaz'ants tank e]

I'll take it.

Ես կվերցնեմ սա:
[yes kvertsn'em sa]

Excuse me, where do I pay?

Ներեցեք, որտե՞ղ է դրամարկղը:
[nerets'eq, vort'egh e dram'arkghy?]

Will you pay in cash or credit card?

Ինչպե՞ս եք վճարելու։
Կանխիկ կ թե քարտով։
[inchp'es eq vcharel'u?
kankh'ik te qart'ov?]

In cash | with credit card

կանխիկ | քարտով
[kankh'ik | qart'ov]

Do you want the receipt?

Ձեզ չեքն անհրաժե՞շտ է։
[dzez cheqn anhrazh'esht e?]

Yes, please.

Այո, խնդրում եմ։
[ay'o, khndrum em]

No, it's OK.

Ոչ, պետք չէ։ Շնորհակալություն։
[voch, petq che. shnorhakaluty'un]

Thank you. Have a nice day!

Շնորհակալություն։ Ցտեսություն։
[shnorhakaluty'un tstesuty'un!]

In town

Excuse me, please.	Ներեցեք խնդրեմ ... [nerets'eq khndrem ...]
I'm looking for ...	Ես փնտրում եմ ... [yes pntrum am ...]

the subway	մետրո [metr'o]
my hotel	իմ հյուրանոցը [im hyuran'otsy]
the movie theater	կինոթատրոն [kinotatr'on]
a taxi stand	տաքսիների կայան [taxiner'i kay'an]

an ATM	բանկոմատ [bankom'at]
a foreign exchange office	արժույթի փոխանակման կետ [arzhuyt'i pvokhanakm'an ket]
an internet café	ինտերնետ-սրճարան [intern'et-srchar'an]
... street	... փողոցը [... pogh'otsy]
this place	այս տեղը ['ays t'eghy]

Do you know where ... is?	Դուք գիտե՞ք որտեղ է գտնվում ...: [duq git'eq vort'egh e gtnv'um ...?]
Which street is this?	Ինչպե՞ս է կոչվում այս փողոցը: [inchp'es e kochv'um ays pvogh'otsy?]

Show me where we are right now.	Ցույց տվեք՝ որտեղ ենք մենք հիմա: [tsuyts tveq vort'egh enq menq him'a]
Can I get there on foot?	Ես կհասնե՞մ այնտեղ ոտքով: [yes khasn'em aynt'egh votq'ov?]
Do you have a map of the city?	Դուք ունե՞ք քաղաքի քարտեզը: [duq un'eq qagh'aqi qart'ezy?]

How much is a ticket to get in?	Որքա՞ն արժե մուտքի տոմսը: [vorq'an arzh'e mutqi t'omsy?]
Can I take pictures here?	Այստեղ կարելի՞ է լուսանկարել: [ayst'egh karel'i e lusankar'el?]
Are you open?	Դուք բա՞ց եք: [duq b'ats eq?]

When do you open?

Ժամը քանիսի՞ն եք դուք բացվում:
[zh'amy qanis'in eq duq batsv'um?]

When do you close?

Մինչև ո՞ր ժամն եք աշխատում:
[minch'ev vor zhamn eq ashkhat'um?]

Money

money	փող [pogh]
cash	կանխիկ դրամ [kankh'ik dram]
paper money	թղթադրամ [tghtadr'am]
loose change	մանրադրամ [manradr'am]
check | change | tip	հաշիվ | մանր | թեյավճար [hash'iv | manr | tyeyavch'ar]
credit card	կրեդիտ քարտ [kred'it qart]
wallet	դրամապանակ [dramapan'ak]
to buy	գնել [gnel]
to pay	վճարել [vchar'el]
fine	տուգանք [tug'anq]
free	անվճար [anvch'ar]
Where can I buy ...?	Որտե՞ղ կարող եմ գնել ...: [vort'egh kar'ogh am gnel ...?]
Is the bank open now?	Բանկը հիմա բա՞ց է: [b'anky him'a bats e?]
When does it open?	Ժամը քանիսի՞ն է այն բացվում: [zh'amy qanis'in e 'ayn batsv'um?]
When does it close?	Մինչև ո՞ր ժամն է այն աշխատում: [minch'ev vor zhamn e 'ayn ashkhat'um?]
How much?	Ինչքա՞ն: [inchq'an?]
How much is this?	Սա ինչքա՞ն արժե: [sa inchq'an arzh'e?]
That's too expensive.	Դա չափազանց թանկ է: [da chapaz'ants tank e]
Excuse me, where do I pay?	Ներեցեք, որտե՞ղ է դրամարկղը: [nerets'eq, vort'egh e dram'arkghy?]
Check, please.	Հաշիվը, խնդրում եմ: [hash'ivy, khndrum em]

Can I pay by credit card?

Կարո՞ղ եմ վճարել քարտով։
[kar'ogh am vchar'el qart'ov?]

Is there an ATM here?

Այստեղ բանկոմատ կա՞։
[ayst'egh bankom'at ka?]

I'm looking for an ATM.

Ինձ բանկոմատ է հարկավոր։
[indz bankom'at e harkav'or?]

I'm looking for a foreign exchange office.

Ես փնտրում եմ փոխանակման կետ։
[yes pntrum am pokhanakm'an ket]

I'd like to change ...

Ես ուզում եմ փոխանակել ...
[yes uz'um am pokhanak'el ...]

What is the exchange rate?

Ասացեք, խնդրեմ, փոխարժեքը։
[asats'eq, khndrem, pokharzh'eqy?]

Do you need my passport?

Ձեզ պե՞տք է իմ անձնագիրը։
[dzez petq e im andznag'iry?]

Time

What time is it?	Ժամը քանի՞սն է: [zh'amy qan'isn e?]
When?	Ե՞րբ: [yerb?]
At what time?	Ժամը քանիսի՞ն: [zh'amy qanis'in?]
now | later | after …	հիմա | ավելի ուշ | …ից հետո [him'a | avel'i ush | …its het'o]
one o'clock	ցերեկվա ժամը մեկը [tserekv'a zh'amy m'eky]
one fifteen	մեկն անց տասնհինգ րոպե [mekn ants tasnh'ing rop'e]
one thirty	մեկն անց կես [m'ekn ants kes]
one forty-five	երկուսին տասնհինգ պակաս [yerkus'in tasnh'ing pak'as]
one | two | three	մեկ | երկու | երեք [mek | yerk'u | yer'ek]
four | five | six	չորս | հինգ | վեց [chors | hing | vets]
seven | eight | nine	յոթ | ութ | ինը [yot | ut | 'iny]
ten | eleven | twelve	տաս | տասնմեկ | տասներկու [tas | tasnm'ek | tasnerk'u]
in …	…ից [….its]
five minutes	հինգ րոպե [hing rop'e]
ten minutes	տաս րոպե [tas rop'e]
fifteen minutes	տասնհինգ րոպե [tasnh'ing rop'e]
twenty minutes	քսան րոպե [qsan rop'e]
half an hour	կես ժամ [kes zham]
an hour	մեկ ժամ [mek zham]

in the morning	առավոտյան [aravoty'an]
early in the morning	վաղ առավոտյան [vagh aravoty'an]
this morning	այսօր առավոտյան [ays'or aravoty'an]
tomorrow morning	վաղն առավոտյան [v'aghn aravoty'an]
at noon	ճաշին [chash'in]
in the afternoon	ճաշից հետո [chash'its het'o]
in the evening	երեկոյան [yerekoy'an]
tonight	այսօր երեկոյան [ays'or yerekoy'an]
at night	գիշերը [gish'ery]
yesterday	երեկ [yer'ek]
today	այսօր [ays'or]
tomorrow	վաղը [v'aghy]
the day after tomorrow	վաղը չէ մյուս օրը [v'aghy che my'us 'ory]
What day is it today?	Շաբաթվա ի՞նչ օր է այսօր: [shabatv'a inch or e ays'or?]
It's ...	Այսօր ... է: [ays'or ... e]
Monday	երկուշաբթի [yerkushabt'i]
Tuesday	երեքշաբթի [yerekshabt'i]
Wednesday	չորեքշաբթի [choreqshabt'i]
Thursday	հինգշաբթի [hingshabt'i]
Friday	ուրբաթ [urb'at]
Saturday	շաբաթ [shab'at]
Sunday	կիրակի [kirak'i]

Greetings. Introductions

Hello.
Բարև Ձեզ:
[bar'ev dzez]

Pleased to meet you.
Ուրախ եմ Ձեզ հետ ծանոթանալու:
[ur'akh am dzez het tsanotanal'u]

Me too.
Նմանապես:
[nmanap'es]

I'd like you to meet ...
Ծանոթացեք: Սա ... է:
[tsanotats'ek. sa ... e]

Nice to meet you.
Շատ հաճելի է:
[shat hachel'i e]

How are you?
Ինչպե՞ս եք: Ինչպե՞ս են Ձեր գործերը:
[inchp'es eq? inchp'es en dzer gorts'ery?]

My name is ...
Իմ անունը ... է:
[im an'uny ... e]

His name is ...
Նրա անունը ... է:
[nra an'uny ... e]

Her name is ...
Նրա անունը ... է:
[nra an'uny ... e]

What's your name?
Ձեր անունն ի՞նչ է:
[dzer an'unn inch e?]

What's his name?
Ի՞նչ է նրա անունը:
[inch e nra an'uny?]

What's her name?
Ի՞նչ է նրա անունը:
[inch e nra an'uny?]

What's your last name?
Ի՞նչ է Ձեր ազգանունը:
[inch e dzer azgan'uny?]

You can call me ...
Ասացեք ինձ ...
[asac'eq indz ...]

Where are you from?
Որտեղի՞ց եք դուք:
[vortegh'its eq duq?]

I'm from ...
Ես ...իցֈ եմ:
[yes ...its am]

What do you do for a living?
Որտե՞ղ եք աշխատում:
[vort'egh eq ashkhat'um?]

Who is this?
Ո՞վ է սա:
[ov e sa?]

Who is he?
Ո՞վ է նա:
[ov e na?]

Who is she?
Ո՞վ է նա:
[ov e na?]

Who are they?
Ո՞վ են նրանք:
[ov en nr'ank?]

This is ...
Սա ...ն է:
[sa ...n e]

my friend (masc.)
իմ ընկեր
[im ynk'er]

my friend (fem.)
իմ ընկերուհի
[im ynkeruh'i]

my husband
իմ ամուսին
[im amus'in]

my wife
իմ կին
[im kin]

my father
իմ հայր
[im hayr]

my mother
իմ մայր
[im mayr]

my brother
իմ եղբայր
[im yeghb'ayr]

my sister
իմ քույր
[im quyr]

my son
իմ որդի
[im vord'i]

my daughter
իմ դուստր
[im dustr]

This is our son.
Սա մեր որդին է:
[sa mer vord'in e]

This is our daughter.
Սա մեր դուստրն է:
[sa mer d'ustrn e]

These are my children.
Սրանք իմ երեխաներն են:
[srank im yerekhan'ern en]

These are our children.
Սրանք մեր երեխաներն են:
[srank mer yerekhan'ern en]

Farewells

Good bye! | Ցտեսություն: [tstesuty'un!]

Bye! (inform.) | Հաջո՛ղ: [haj'ogh!]

See you tomorrow. | Մինչ վաղը: [minch v'aghy]

See you soon. | Մինչ հանդիպում: [minch handip'um]

See you at seven. | Կհանդիպենք ժամը յոթին: [khandip'enk zh'amy yot'in]

Have fun! | Զվարճացեք: [zvarchats'eq!]

Talk to you later. | Հետո կխոսենք: [het'o kkhos'enq]

Have a nice weekend. | Հաջող հանգստյան օրեր եմ ցանկանում: [haj'ogh hangsty'an or'er am tsankan'um]

Good night. | Բարի գիշեր: [bar'i gish'er]

It's time for me to go. | Գնալուս ժամանակն է: [gnal'us zhaman'akn e]

I have to go. | Ես պետք է գնամ: [yes petq e gnam]

I will be right back. | Ես հիմա կվերադառնամ: [yes him'a kveradarn'am]

It's late. | Արդեն ուշ է: [ard'en 'ush e]

I have to get up early. | Ես պետք է վաղ արթնանամ: [yes petq e vagh artnan'am]

I'm leaving tomorrow. | Ես վաղը մեկնում եմ: [yes v'aghy mekn'um am]

We're leaving tomorrow. | Մենք վաղը մեկնում ենք: [menq v'aghy mekn'um enq]

Have a nice trip! | Բարի ճանապա՜րհ: [bar'i chanap'arh!]

It was nice meeting you. | Հաճելի էր ձեզ հետ ծանոթանալ: [hachel'i er dzez het tsanotan'al]

It was nice talking to you. | Հաճելի էր ձեզ հետ շփվել: [hachel'i er dzez het shpv'el]

Thanks for everything. | Շնորհակալություն ամեն ինչի համար: [shnorhakaluty'un am'en inch'i ham'ar]

I had a very good time.	Ես հոյակապ անցկացրեցի ժամանակը: [yes hoyak'ap antskatsrets'i zhaman'aky]
We had a very good time.	Մենք հոյակապ անցկացրեցինք ժամանակը: [menq hoyak'ap antskatsrets'inq zhaman'aky]
It was really great.	Ամեն ինչ հոյակապ էր: [am'en inch hoyak'ap er]
I'm going to miss you.	Ես կկարոտեմ: [yes kkarot'em]
We're going to miss you.	Մենք կկարոտենք: [menq kkarot'enq]

Good luck!	Հաջողությո՜ւն: Մնաք բարո՜վ: [hajoghuty'un! mnaq baro'v!]
Say hi to ...	Բարևեք ...ին: [barev'eq ...in]

Foreign language

| I don't understand. | Ես չեմ հասկանում: |
| | [yes chem haskan'um] |

Write it down, please.
Մնդրում եմ, գրեք դա:
[khndrum em, greq da]

Do you speak ...?
Դուք գիտե՞ք ...:
[duq git'eq ...?]

I speak a little bit of ...
Ես գիտեմ մի քիչ ...
[yes git'em mi qich ...]

English
անգլերեն
[angler'en]

Turkish
թուրքերեն
[turker'en]

Arabic
արաբերեն
[araber'en]

French
ֆրանսերեն
[franser'en]

German
գերմաներեն
[germaner'en]

Italian
իտալերեն
[italer'en]

Spanish
իսպաներեն
[ispaner'en]

Portuguese
պորտուգալերեն
[portugaler'en]

Chinese
չինարեն
[chiner'en]

Japanese
ճապոներեն
[chaponer'en]

Can you repeat that, please.
Կրկնեք, խնդրեմ:
[krkneq, khndrem]

I understand.
Ես հասկանում եմ:
[yes haskan'um am]

I don't understand.
Ես չեմ հասկանում:
[yes chem haskan'um]

Please speak more slowly.
Խոսեք դանդաղ, խնդրում եմ:
[khos'eq dand'agh, khndrum em]

Is that correct? (Am I saying it right?)
Սա ճի՞շտ է:
[sa chisht e?]

What is this? (What does this mean?)
Ի՞նչ է սա:
[inch e sa?]

Apologies

Excuse me, please.	Ներեցեք, խնդրեմ: [nerets'eq, khndrem]
I'm sorry.	Ցավում եմ: [tsav'um am]
I'm really sorry.	Շատ ափսոս: [shat aps'os]
Sorry, it's my fault.	Իմ մեղավորությունն է: [im meghavoruty'unn e]
My mistake.	Իմ սխալն է: [im skh'aln e]
May I ...?	Ես կարո՞ղ եմ ...: [yes kar'ogh am ...?]
Do you mind if I ...?	Դեմ չե՞ք լինի, եթե ես ...: [dem cheq lini, yet'e yes ...?]
It's OK.	Սարսափելի ոչինչ չկա: [sarsap'eli voch'inch chka]
It's all right.	Ամեն ինչ կարգին է: [am'en inch karg'in e]
Don't worry about it.	Մի անհանգստացեք: [mi anhangstats'eq]

Agreement

Yes.	Այո: [ay'o]
Yes, sure.	Այո, իհարկե: [ay'o, ih'arke]
OK (Good!)	Լա́վ: [lav!]
Very well.	Շատ լավ: [shat lav]
Certainly!	Իհարկե: [ih'arke]
I agree.	Ես համաձայն եմ: [yes hamadz'ayn am]

That's correct.	Ճիշտ է: [chisht e]
That's right.	Ճիշտ է: [chisht e]
You're right.	Դուք իրավացի եք: [duq iravats'i eq]
I don't mind.	Ես չեմ առարկում: [yes chem arark'um]
Absolutely right.	Բացարձակ ճիշտ է: [batsardz'ak ch'isht e]

It's possible.	Հնարավոր է: [hnarav'or e]
That's a good idea.	Լավ միտք է: [lav mitq e]
I can't say no.	Չեմ կարող մերժել: [chem kar'ogh merzh'el]
I'd be happy to.	Ուրախ կլինեմ: [ur'akh klin'em]
With pleasure.	Հաճույքով: [hachuyq'ov]

Refusal. Expressing doubt

No.	Ոչ: [voch]
Certainly not.	Իհարկե, ոչ: [ih'arke, voch]
I don't agree.	Ես համաձայն չեմ: [yes hamadz'ayn chem]
I don't think so.	Ես այդպես չեմ կարծում: [yes ayes chem karts'um]
It's not true.	Սուտ է: [sut e]
You are wrong.	Դուք իրավացի չեք: [duq iravats'i cheq]
I think you are wrong.	Կարծում եմ՝ իրավացի չեք: [karts'um am iravats'i cheq]
I'm not sure.	Համոզված չեմ: [hamozv'ats chem]
It's impossible.	Անհնար է: [anhn'ar e]
Nothing of the kind (sort)!	Ո՛չ մի նման բան: [voch mi nman ban]
The exact opposite.	Հակառակը: [hakar'aky]
I'm against it.	Ես դեմ եմ: [yes dem am]
I don't care.	Ինձ միեւնույն է: [indz mievn'uyn e]
I have no idea.	Գաղափար չունեմ: [gaghap'ar chun'em]
I doubt that.	Կասկածում եմ, որ այդպես է: [kaskats'um am, vor aydp'es e]
Sorry, I can't.	Ներեցեք, չեմ կարող: [nerets'eq, chem kar'ogh]
Sorry, I don't want to.	Ներեցեք, չեմ ուզում: [nerets'eq, chem uz'um]
Thank you, but I don't need this.	Շնորհակալություն, ինձ պետք չէ: [shnorhakaluty'un, indz petq che]
It's late.	Արդեն ուշ է: [ard'en 'ush e]

I have to get up early.

Ես պետք է վաղ արթնանամ։
[yes petq e vagh artnan'am]

I don't feel well.

Ես ինձ վատ եմ զգում։
[indz vat am zgum]

Expressing gratitude

Thank you.
Շնորհակալություն։
[shnorhakaluty'un]

Thank you very much.
Շատ շնորհակալ եմ։
[shat shnorhak'al am]

I really appreciate it.
Շատ շնորհակալ եմ։
[shat shnorhak'al am]

I'm really grateful to you.
Շնորհակալ եմ։
[shnorhak'al am]

We are really grateful to you.
Շնորհակալ ենք։
[shnorhak'al enq]

Thank you for your time.
Շնորհակալություն, որ ձախսեցիք ձեր ժամանակը։
[shnorhakaluty'un, vor tsakhsets'ik dzer zhaman'aky]

Thanks for everything.
Շնորհակալություն ամեն ինչի համար։
[shnorhakaluty'un am'en inch'i ham'ar]

Thank you for ...
Շնորհակալություն ... համար։
[shnorhakaluty'un ... ham'ar]

your help
ձեր օգնության
[dzer ognuty'an]

a nice time
լավ ժամանցի
[lav zhamants'i]

a wonderful meal
հոյակապ ուտեստների
[hoyak'ap utestner'i]

a pleasant evening
հաճելի երեկոյի
[hachel'l erekoy'i]

a wonderful day
հիանալի օրվա
[hianal'i orv'a]

an amazing journey
հետաքրքիր էքսկուրսիայի
[hetaqrq'ir eqskursiay'i]

Don't mention it.
Չարժե։
[charzh'e]

You are welcome.
Չարժե։
[charzh'e]

Any time.
Միշտ խնդրեմ։
[misht khndrem]

My pleasure.
Ուրախ էի օգնելու։
[ur'akh ei ognel'u]

Forget it. It's alright.   **Մոռացեք:**
[morats'eq]

Don't worry about it.   **Մի անհանգստացեք:**
[mi anhangstats'eq]

Congratulations. Best wishes

Congratulations!

Շնորհավորում եմ:
[shnorhavor'um am!]

Happy birthday!

Շնորհավոր ծննդյան օրը:
[shnorhav'or tsnndy'an 'ory!]

Merry Christmas!

Շնորհավոր Սուրբ ծնունդ:
[shnorhav'or surb tsnund!]

Happy New Year!

Շնորհավոր Ամանոր:
[shnorhav'or aman'or!]

Happy Easter!

Շնորհավոր Զատիկ:
[shnorhav'or zat'ik!]

Happy Hanukkah!

Ուրախ Հանուկա:
[ur'akh h'anuka!]

I'd like to propose a toast.

Ես կենաց ունեմ:
[yes ken'ats un'em]

Cheers!

Ձեր առողջության կենացը:
[dzer aroghjuty'an ken'atsy!]

Let's drink to …!

Խմենք … համար:
[khmenq … ham'ar!]

To our success!

Մեր հաջողության կենացը:
[mer hajoghuty'an ken'atsy!]

To your success!

Ձեր հաջողության կենացը:
[dzer hajoghuty'an ken'atsy!]

Good luck!

Հաջողություն:
[hajoghuty'un!]

Have a nice day!

Հաճելի օր եմ ցանկանում:
[hachel'i 'or am tsankan'um!]

Have a good holiday!

Հաճելի հանգիստ եմ ցանկանում:
[hachel'I hang'ist am tsankan'um!]

Have a safe journey!

Բարի ճանապարհ:
[bar'i chanap'arh!]

I hope you get better soon!

Շուտ ապաքինում եմ ցանկանում:
[shut apaqin'um am cankan'um!]

Socializing

Why are you sad?	Ինչո՞ւ եք տխրել: [inxh'u eq tkhrel?]
Smile! Cheer up!	Ժպտացե՛ք: [zhptatsy'ek!]
Are you free tonight?	Դուք զբաղվա՞ծ եք այսոր երեկոյան: [duq zbaghv'ats eq ays'or yerekoy'an?]
May I offer you a drink?	Կարո՞ղ եմ առաջարկել ձեզ որևէ ըմպելիք: [kar'ogh am arajark'el dzez vorev'e ympel'iq?]
Would you like to dance?	Չե՞ք ցանկանա պարել: [cheq tsankan'a par'el?]
Let's go to the movies.	Գնա՞նք կինոթատրոն: [gnanq kinotatr'on?]
May I invite you to ...?	Կարո՞ղ եմ հրավիրել ձեզ ...: [kar'ogh am hravir'el dzez ...?]
a restaurant	ռեստորան [rrestor'an]
the movies	կինոթատրոն [kinotatr'on]
the theater	թատրոն [tatr'on]
go for a walk	զբոսանքի [zbosanq'i]
At what time?	Ժամը քանիսի՞ն: [zh'amy qanis'in?]
tonight	այսոր երեկոյան [ays'or yerekoy'an]
at six	ժամը վեցին [zh'amy vec'in]
at seven	ժամը յոթին [zh'amy yot'in]
at eight	ժամը ութին [zh'amy out'in]
at nine	ժամը իննին [zh'amy inn'in]
Do you like it here?	Ձեզ այստեղ դու՞ր է գալիս: [dzez ayst'egh dur e gal'is?]
Are you here with someone?	Դուք այստեղ ինչ-որ մեկի հե՞տ եք: [duq ayst'egh 'inch-vor mek'i het eq?]

I'm with my friend.	Ես ընկերոջս /ընկերուհիու/ հետ եմ:
	[yes ynker'ojs /ynkeruh'us/ het am]
I'm with my friends.	Ես ընկերներիս հետ եմ:
	[yes ynkerner'is het am]
No, I'm alone.	Ես մենակ եմ:
	[yes men'ak am]

Do you have a boyfriend?	Դու ընկեր ունե՞ս:
	[du ynk'er un'es?]
I have a boyfriend.	Ես ընկեր ունեմ:
	[yes ynk'er un'em]
Do you have a girlfriend?	Դու ընկերուհի ունե՞ս:
	[du ynkeruh'i un'es?]
I have a girlfriend.	Ես ընկերուհի ունեմ:
	[yes ynkeruh'i un'em]

Can I see you again?	Մենք դեռ կհանդիպե՞նք:
	[menq der khandip'enq?]
Can I call you?	Կարո՞ղ եմ քեզ զանգահարել:
	[kar'ogh am qez zangahar'el?]
Call me. (Give me a call.)	Կզանգես:
	[kzang'es]
What's your number?	Ո՞նց է համարդ
	[vonts e ham'ard?]
I miss you.	Ես կարոտում եմ քեզ:
	[yes karot'um am qez]

You have a beautiful name.	Դուք շատ գեղեցիկ անուն ունեք:
	[duq shat geghets'ik an'un un'eq]
I love you.	Ես սիրում եմ քեզ:
	[yes sir'um am qez]
Will you marry me?	Արի՛ ամուսնանանք:
	[ar'i amusnan'anq]
You're kidding!	Դուք կատակում եք:
	[duq katak'um eq!]
I'm just kidding.	Ես ուղղակի կատակում եմ:
	[yes ughghak'i katak'um am]

Are you serious?	Դուք լո՞ւրջ եք ասում:
	[duq l'urj eq as'um?]
I'm serious.	Ես լուրջ եմ ասում:
	[yes lurj am as'um]
Really?!	Իրո՞ք:
	[ir'oq?!]
It's unbelievable!	Դա անհավանական է:
	[da anhavanak'an e!]
I don't believe you.	Ես ձեզ չեմ հավատում:
	[yes dzez chem havat'um]
I can't.	Ես չեմ կարող:
	[yes chem kar'ogh]
I don't know.	Ես չգիտեմ:
	[yes chgit'em]

I don't understand you.

Ես Ձեզ չեմ հասկանում:
[yes dzez chem haskan'um]

Please go away.

Հեռացեք, խնդրում եմ:
[herats'ek, khndrum em]

Leave me alone!

Ինձ հանգի´ստ թողեք:
[indz hang'ist togh'eq]

I can't stand him.

Ես նրան տանել չեմ կարողանում:
[yes nran tan'el chem karoghan'um]

You are disgusting!

Դուք զզվելի եք:
[duq zzvel'i eq!]

I'll call the police!

Ես ոստիկանություն կկանչեմ:
[yes vostikanuty'un kkanch'em!]

Sharing impressions. Emotions

I like it.	Ինձ դա դուր է գալիս: [indz da dur e gal'is]
Very nice.	Հաճելի է: [hachel'i e]
That's great!	Հրաշալի է: [hrashal'i e!]
It's not bad.	Վատ չէ: [vat che]
I don't like it.	Սա ինձ դուր է գալիս: [indz dur e gal'is]
It's not good.	Դա լավ չի: [da lav chi]
It's bad.	Դա վատ է: [da vat e]
It's very bad.	Դա շատ վատ է: [da shat vat e]
It's disgusting.	Զզվելի է: [zzvel'i e]
I'm happy.	Ես երջանիկ եմ: [yes yerjan'ik am]
I'm content.	Ես գոհ եմ: [yes goh am]
I'm in love.	Ես սիրահարվել եմ: [yes siraharv'el am]
I'm calm.	Ես հանգիստ եմ: [yes hang'ist am]
I'm bored.	Ես ձանձրանում եմ: [yes dzandzran'um am]
I'm tired.	Ես հոգնել եմ: [yes hogn'el am]
I'm sad.	Ես տխուր եմ: [yes tkhur am]
I'm frightened.	Ես վախեցած եմ: [yes vakhets'ats am]
I'm angry.	Ես զայրանում եմ: [yes zayran'um am]
I'm worried.	Ես անհանգստանում եմ: [yes anhangstan'um am]
I'm nervous.	Ես ջղայնանում եմ: [yes jghaynan'um am]

I'm jealous. (envious)

Ես նախանձում եմ:
[yes nakhandz'um am]

I'm surprised.

Ես զարմացած եմ:
[yes zarmats'ats am]

I'm perplexed.

Ես շփոթված եմ:
[yes shpvotv'ats am]

Problems. Accidents

I've got a problem. | Ես խնդիր ունեմ:
[yes khndir un'em]

We've got a problem. | Մենք խնդիրներ ունենք:
[menq khndirn'er un'enq]

I'm lost. | Ես մոլորվել եմ:
[yes molorv'el am]

I missed the last bus (train). | Ես ուշացել եմ վերջին ավտոբուսից (գնացքից):
[yes ushats'el am verj'in avtob'usits (gnatsq'its)]

I don't have any money left. | Ինձ մոտ դրամ ընդհանրապես չի մնացել:
[indz mot dram yndhanrap'es chi mnats'el]

I've lost my ... | Ես կորցրել եմ ...
[yes kortsr'el am ...]

Someone stole my ... | Ինձ մոտից գողացել են ...
[indz mot'its goghats'el en ...]

passport | անձնագիրը
[andznag'iry]

wallet | դրամապանակը
[dramapan'aky]

papers | փաստաթղթերը
[pastatght'ery]

ticket | տոմսը
[t'omsy]

money | փողը
[p'oghy]

handbag | պայուսակը
[payus'aky]

camera | ֆոտոապարատը
[fotoapar'aty]

laptop | նոութբուքը
[noteb'ooky]

tablet computer | պլանշետը
[plansh'ety]

mobile phone | հեռախոսը
[herakh'osy]

Help me! | Օգնեցե՜ք:
[ognets'eq!]

What's happened? | Ի՞նչ է պատահել:
[inch e patah'el?]

fire	հրդեհ
	[hrdeh]
shooting	կրակոց
	[krak'ots]
murder	սպանություն
	[spanuty'un]
explosion	պայթյուն
	[payty'un]
fight	կռիվ
	[kriv]

Call the police!	Ոստիկանություն կանչեք:
	[vostikanuty'un kanch'eq!]
Please hurry up!	Արագացրեք, խնդրում եմ:
	[aragatsr'eq, khndrum em!]
I'm looking for the police station.	Ես փնտրում եմ ոստիկանության բաժին
	[yes pntrum am vostikanuty'an bazh'in]
I need to make a call.	Ինձ պետք է զանգահարել:
	[indz petq e zangahar'el]
May I use your phone?	Կարո՞ղ եմ զանգահարել:
	[kar'ogh am zangahar'el?]

I've been ...	Ինձ ...
	[indz ...]
mugged	կողոպտել են
	[koghopt'el en]
robbed	թալանել են
	[talan'el en]
raped	բռնաբարել են
	[brnabar'el en]
attacked (beaten up)	ծեծել են
	[tsets'el en]

Are you all right?	Ձեզ հետ ամեն ինչ կարգի՞ն է:
	[dzez het am'en inch karg'in e?]
Did you see who it was?	Դուք տեսե՞լ եք, ով էր նա:
	[duq tes'el eq, ov er na?]
Would you be able to recognize the person?	Կարո՞ղ եք նրան ճանաչել:
	[kar'ogh eq nran chanach'el?]
Are you sure?	Համոզվա՞ծ եք:
	[hamozv'ats eq?]

Please calm down.	Խնդրում եմ, հանգստացեք:
	[khndrum em, hangstats'eq]
Take it easy!	Հանգիստ:
	[hang'ist!]
Don't worry!	Մի անհանգստացեք:
	[mi anhangstats'eq]
Everything will be fine.	Ամեն ինչ լավ կլինի:
	[am'en inch lav klin'i]
Everything's all right.	Ամեն ինչ կարգին է:
	[am'en inch karg'in e]

Come here, please.

Մոտեցեք, խնդրեմ:
[motets'eq, khndrem]

I have some questions for you.

Ես ձեզ մի քանի հարց ունեմ տալու:
[yes dzez mi qan'i harts un'em tal'u]

Wait a moment, please.

Սպասեք, խնդրեմ:
[spas'eq, khndrem]

Do you have any I.D.?

Դուք փաստաթղթեր ունե՞ք:
[duq pastatght'er un'eq?]

Thanks. You can leave now.

Շնորհակալություն:
Դուք կարող եք գնալ:
[shnorhakaluty'un.
duq kar'ogh eq gnal]

Hands behind your head!

Ձերքերը գլխի հետև՛:
[dzerk'ery glkhi het'ev!]

You're under arrest!

Դուք ձերբակալվա՞ծ եք:
[duq dzerbakalv'ats eq!]

Health problems

Please help me.	Oգնեցեք, խնդրում եմ: [ognets'eq, khndrum em]
I don't feel well.	Ես ինձ վատ եմ զգում: [yes indz vat am zgum]
My husband doesn't feel well.	Իմ ամուսինն իրեն վատ է զգում: [im amus'inn ir'en vat e zgum]
My son ...	Իմ որդին ... [im vord'in ...]
My father ...	Իմ հայրն ... [im hayrn ...]
My wife doesn't feel well.	Իմ կինն իրեն վատ է զգում: [im kinn ir'en vat e zgum]
My daughter ...	Իմ դուստրն ... [im dustrn ...]
My mother ...	Իմ մայրն ... [im mayrn ...]
I've got a ...	Իմ ... ցավում է: [im ... tsav'um e]
headache	գլուխը [gl'ukhy]
sore throat	կոկորդը [kok'ordy]
stomach ache	փորը [p'ory]
toothache	ատամը [at'amy]
I feel dizzy.	Գլուխս պտտվում է: [glukhs pttvum e]
He has a fever.	Նա ջերմություն ունի: [na jermuty'un un'i]
She has a fever.	Նա ջերմություն ունի: [na jermuty'un un'i]
I can't breathe.	Ես չեմ կարողանում շնչել: [yes chem karoghan'um shnch'el]
I'm short of breath.	Խեղդվում եմ: [kheghdv'um am]
I am asthmatic.	Ես աստմահար եմ: [yes astmah'ar am]
I am diabetic.	Ես շաքարախտ ունեմ: [yes shakar'akht un'em]

English	Armenian
I can't sleep.	Ես անքնություն ունեմ: [yes anknuty'un un'em]
food poisoning	սննդային թունավորում [snnday'in tunavor'um]
It hurts here.	Այստեղ է ցավում: [ayst'egh e tsav'um]
Help me!	Օգնեցե՛ք: [ognets'eq!]
I am here!	Ես այստեղ եմ: [yes ayst'egh am!]
We are here!	Մենք այստեղ ենք: [menq ayst'egh enq!]
Get me out of here!	Հանեք ինձ: [khan'ek indz!]
I need a doctor.	Ինձ բժիշկ է պետք: [indz bzhishk e petq]
I can't move.	Ես չեմ կարողանում շարժվել: [yes chem karoghan'um sharzhv'el]
I can't move my legs.	Ես չեմ զգում ոտքերս: [yes chem zgum votq'ers]
I have a wound.	Ես վիրավոր եմ: [yes virav'or am]
Is it serious?	Լո՞ւրջ: [lurj?]
My documents are in my pocket.	Իմ փաստաթղթերը գրպանումս են: [im pastatght'ery grpan'ums en]
Calm down!	Հանգստացեք: [hangstats'eq!]
May I use your phone?	Կարո՞ղ եմ զանգահարել: [kar'ogh am zangahar'el?]
Call an ambulance!	Շտապ օգնություն կանչեք: [shtap ognuty'un kanch'eq!]
It's urgent!	Սա շտապ է: [sa shtap e!]
It's an emergency!	Սա շատ շտապ է: [sa shat shtap e!]
Please hurry up!	Արագացրեք, խնդրում եմ: [aragatsr'eq, khndrum em!]
Would you please call a doctor?	Բժիշկ կանչեք, խնդրում եմ: [bzhishk kanch'eq, khndrum em]
Where is the hospital?	Ասացեք, որտե՞ղ է հիվանդանոցը: [asats'eq, vort'egh e hivandan'otsy?]
How are you feeling?	Ինչպե՞ս եք ձեզ զգում: [inchp'es eq dzez zgum?]
Are you all right?	Ձեզ հետ ամեն ինչ կարգի՞ն է: [dzez het am'en inch karg'in e?]
What's happened?	Ի՞նչ է պատահել: [inch e patah'el?]

I feel better now.   Ես արդեն ինձ լավ եմ զգում։
                                        [indz lav am zgum]

It's OK.   Ամեն ինչ կարգին է։
                                        [am'en inch karg'in e]

It's all right.   Ամեն ինչ լավ է։
                                        [am'en inch l'av e]

At the pharmacy

pharmacy (drugstore)	դեղատուն [deghat'un]
24-hour pharmacy	շուրջօրյա դեղատուն [shurjory'a deghat'un]
Where is the closest pharmacy?	Որտե՞ղ է մոտակա դեղատունը: [vort'egh e motak'a deghat'uny?]
Is it open now?	Այն հիմա բա՞ց է: [ayn him'a bats e?]
At what time does it open?	Ժամը քանիսի՞ն է այն բացվում: [zh'amy qanis'in e 'ayn batsv'um?]
At what time does it close?	Մինչև ո՞ր ժամն է այն աշխատում: [minch'ev vor zhamn e 'ayn ashkhat'um?]
Is it far?	Դա հեռու՞ է: [da her'u e?]
Can I get there on foot?	Ես կհասնե՞մ այնտեղ ոտքով: [yes khasn'em aynt'egh votq'ov?]
Can you show me on the map?	Ցույց տվեք ինձ քարտեզի վրա, խնդրում եմ: [tsuyts tveq indz qartez'i vra, khndrum am]
Please give me something for …	Տվեք ինձ ինչ-որ բան … համար: [tveq indz inch-v'or ban … ham'ar]
a headache	գլխացավի [glkhatsav'i]
a cough	հազի [haz'i]
a cold	մրսածության [mrsatsuty'an]
the flu	հարբուխի [harbukh'i]
a fever	ջերմության [jermuty'an]
a stomach ache	փորացավի [poratsav'i]
nausea	սրտխառնոցի [srtkharnots'i]
diarrhea	լուծի [luts'i]
constipation	փորկապության [porkaputy'an]

pain in the back	մեջքի ցավ [mejk'i tsav]
chest pain	կրծքի ցավ [krtski tsav]
side stitch	կողացav [koghats'av]
abdominal pain	փորացav [porats'av]

pill	հաբ [hab]
ointment, cream	քսուք, կրեմ [ksuk, krem]
syrup	օշարակ [oshar'ak]
spray	սփրեյ [spr'ay]
drops	կաթիլներ [katiln'er]

You need to go to the hospital.	Դուք պետք է հիվանդանոց գնաք: [duq petq e hivandan'ots gna]
health insurance	ապահովագրություն [apahovagruty'un]
prescription	դեղատոմս [deghat'oms]
insect repellant	միջատների դեմ միջոց [mijatner'i dem mij'ots]
Band Aid	լեյկոսպեղանի [leykospeghan'i]

The bare minimum

Excuse me, ...
Ներեցեք, ...
[nerets'eq, ...]

Hello.
Բարև Ձեզ:
[barev dzez]

Thank you.
Շնորհակալություն:
[shnorhakaluty'un]

Good bye.
Ցտեսություն:
[tstesuty'un]

Yes.
Այո:
[ay'o]

No.
Ոչ:
[voch]

I don't know.
Ես չգիտեմ:
[yes chgit'em]

Where? | Where to? | When?
Ո՞րտեղ: Ո՞ւր: Ե՞րբ:
[vort'egh? ur? yerb?]

I need ...
Ինձ հարկավոր է ...
[indz harkav'or e ...]

I want ...
Ես ուզում եմ ...
[yes uz'um em ...]

Do you have ...?
Դուք ունե՞ք ...:
[duq un'eq ...?]

Is there a ... here?
Այստեղ կա՞ ...:
[ayst'egh ka ...?]

May I ...?
Ես կարո՞ղ եմ ...:
[yes kar'ogh em ...?]

..., please (polite request)
Խնդրում եմ
[khndrum em]

I'm looking for ...
Ես փնտրում եմ ...
[yes pntrum am ...]

restroom
զուգարան
[zugar'an]

ATM
բանկոմատ
[bankom'at]

pharmacy (drugstore)
դեղատուն
[deghat'un]

hospital
հիվանդանոց
[hivandan'ots]

police station
ոստիկանության բաժանմունք
[vostikanuty'an bazhanm'unq]

subway
մետրո
[metr'o]

taxi	տաքսի [tax'i]
train station	կայարան [kayar'an]

My name is ...	Իմ անունը ... է: [im an'uny ... e]
What's your name?	Ձեր անունն ի՞նչ է: [dzer an'unn inch e?]
Could you please help me?	Օգնեցեք ինձ, խնդրեմ: [ognets'eq indz, khndrem]
I've got a problem.	Ես խնդիր ունեմ: [yes khndir un'em]
I don't feel well.	Ես ինձ վատ եմ զգում: [yes indz vat am zgum]
Call an ambulance!	Շտապ օգնություն կանչեք: [shtap ognuty'un kanch'eq!]
May I make a call?	Կարո՞ղ եմ զանգահարել: [kar'ogh am zangahar'el?]

I'm sorry.	Ներեցեք [nerets'eq]
You're welcome.	Խնդրեմ [kndrem]

I, me	Ես [yes]
you (inform.)	դու [du]
he	նա [na]
she	նա [na]
they (masc.)	նրանք [nrank]
they (fem.)	նրանք [nrank]
we	մենք [menq]
you (pl)	դուք [duq]
you (sg, form.)	Դուք [duq]

ENTRANCE	ՄՈՒՏՔ [mutq]
EXIT	ԵԼՔ [yelq]
OUT OF ORDER	ՉԻ ԱՇԽԱՏՈՒՄ [chi ashkhat'um]
CLOSED	ՓԱԿ Է [pak e]

OPEN

ԲԱՑ Է
[bats e]

FOR WOMEN

ԿԱՆԱՆՑ ՀԱՄԱՐ
[kan'ants ham'ar]

FOR MEN

ՏՂԱՄԱՐԴԿԱՆՑ ՀԱՄԱՐ
[tghamardk'ants ham'ar]

MINI DICTIONARY

This section contains 250 useful words required for everyday communication. You will find the names of months and days of the week here. The dictionary also contains topics such as colors, measurements, family, and more

T&P Books Publishing

DICTIONARY CONTENTS

T&P Books Publishing

time	ժամանակ	[ʒama'nak]
hour	ժամ	[ʒam]
half an hour	կես ժամ	[kes 'ʒam]
minute	րոպե	[ro'pɛ]
second	վայրկյան	[vajr'kian]
today (adv)	այսօր	[aj'sor]
tomorrow (adv)	վաղը	['vahı]
yesterday (adv)	երեկ	[e'rek]
Monday	երկուշաբթի	[erkuʃʌb'ti]
Tuesday	երեքշաբթի	[erekʃʌb'ti]
Wednesday	չորեքշաբթի	[tʃorekʃʌb'ti]
Thursday	հինգշաբթի	[inʃʌb'ti]
Friday	ուրբաթ	[ur'bat]
Saturday	շաբաթ	[ʃʌ'bat]
Sunday	կիրակի	[kira'ki]
day	օր	[or]
working day	աշխատանքային օր	[aʃhataŋka'jın 'or]
public holiday	տոնական օր	[tona'kan 'or]
weekend	շաբաթ, կիրակի	[ʃʌ'bat], [kira'ki]
week	շաբաթ	[ʃʌ'bat]
last week (adv)	անցյալ շաբաթ	[an'tsial ʃʌ'bat]
next week (adv)	հաջորդ շաբաթ	[a'dʒort 'orı]
in the morning	առավոտյան	[aravo'tian]
in the afternoon	ճաշից հետո	[tʃa'ʃits ɛ'to]
in the evening	երեկոյան	[ereko'jan]
tonight (this evening)	այսօր երեկոյան	[aj'sor ereko'jan]
at night	գիշերը	[gi'ʃerı]
midnight	կեսգիշեր	[kesgi'ʃer]
January	հունվար	[un'var]
February	փետրվար	[petr'var]
March	մարտ	[mart]
April	ապրիլ	[ap'ril]
May	մայիս	[ma'jıs]
June	հունիս	[u'nis]
July	հուլիս	[u'lis]
August	օգոստոս	[ogos'tos]

September	սեպտեմբեր	[septem'ber]
October	հոկտեմբեր	[oktem'ber]
November	նոյեմբեր	[noem'ber]
December	դեկտեմբեր	[dektem'ber]

in spring	գարնանը	[gar'nanı]
in summer	ամռանը	[am'ranı]
in fall	աշնանը	[aʃ'nanı]
in winter	ձմռանը	[dzm'ranı]

month	ամիս	[a'mis]
season (summer, etc.)	սեզոն	[se'zon]
year	տարի	[ta'ri]

2. Numbers. Numerals

0 zero	զրո	[zro]
1 one	մեկ	[mek]
2 two	երկու	[er'ku]
3 three	երեք	[e'rek]
4 four	չորս	[tʃors]

5 five	հինգ	[hiŋ]
6 six	վեց	[vets]
7 seven	յոթ	[jot]
8 eight	ութ	[ut]
9 nine	ինը	['inɛ]
10 ten	տաս	[tas]

11 eleven	տասնմեկ	[tasn'mek]
12 twelve	տասներկու	[tasner'ku]
13 thirteen	տասներեք	[tasne'rek]
14 fourteen	տասնչորս	[tasn'tʃors]
15 fifteen	տասնհինգ	[tas'niŋ]

16 sixteen	տասնվեց	[tasn'vets]
17 seventeen	տասնյոթ	[tasn'jot]
18 eighteen	տասնութ	[tas'nut]
19 nineteen	տասնինը	[tas'ninɛ]

20 twenty	քսան	[ksan]
30 thirty	երեսուն	[ere'sun]
40 forty	քառասուն	[kara'sun]
50 fifty	հիսուն	[i'sun]

60 sixty	վաթսուն	[va'tsun]
70 seventy	յոթանասուն	[jotana'sun]
80 eighty	ութսուն	[u'tsun]
90 ninety	իննսուն	[iŋ'sun]
100 one hundred	հարյուր	[ar'jur]

200 two hundred	երկու հարյուր	[er'ku ar'jur]
300 three hundred	երեք հարյուր	[e'rek ar'jur]
400 four hundred	չորս հարյուր	['tʃors ar'jur]
500 five hundred	հինգ հարյուր	['hiŋ ar'jur]
600 six hundred	վեց հարյուր	['vets ar'jur]
700 seven hundred	յոթ հարյուր	['jot ar'jur]
800 eight hundred	ութ հարյուր	['ut ar'jur]
900 nine hundred	ինը հարյուր	['inɛ ar'jur]
1000 one thousand	հազար	[a'zar]
10000 ten thousand	տաս հազար	['tas a'zar]
one hundred thousand	հարյուր հազար	[ar'jur a'zar]
million	միլիոն	[mili'on]
billion	միլիարդ	[mili'ard]

3. Humans. Family

man (adult male)	տղամարդ	[tha'mard]
young man	պատանի	[pata'ni]
woman	կին	[kin]
girl (young woman)	օրիորդ	[ori'ord]
old man	ծերունի	[tseru'ni]
old woman	պառավ	[pa'rav]
mother	մայր	[majr]
father	հայր	[ajr]
son	որդի	[vor'di]
daughter	դուստր	[dustr]
brother	եղբայր	[eh'bajr]
sister	քույր	[kujr]
parents	ծնողներ	[tsnoh'ner]
child	երեխա	[ere'ha]
children	երեխաներ	[ereha'ner]
stepmother	խորթ մայր	[hort 'majr]
stepfather	խորթ հայր	[hort 'ajr]
grandmother	տատիկ	[ta'tik]
grandfather	պապիկ	[pa'pik]
grandson	թոռ	[tor]
granddaughter	թոռնուհի	[tornu'i]
grandchildren	թոռներ	[tor'ner]
nephew	քրոջորդի, քրոջ աղջիկ	[krodʒor'di], [k'rodʒ ah'dʒik]
niece	եղբորորդի, եղբոր աղջիկ	[ehbror'di, eh'bor ah'dʒik]
wife	կին	[kin]
husband	ամուսին	[amu'sin]

married (masc.)	ամուսնացած	[amusna'tsats]
married (fem.)	ամուսնացած	[amusna'tsats]
widow	այրի կին	[aj'ri 'kin]
widower	այրի տղամարդ	[aj'ri tha'mard]

name (first name)	անուն	[a'nun]
surname (last name)	ազգանուն	[azga'nun]

relative	ազգական	[azga'kan]
friend (masc.)	ընկեր	[ɪ'ŋker]
friendship	ընկերություն	[ɪŋkeru'tsyn]

partner	գործընկեր	[gortsɪ'ŋker]
superior (n)	պետ	[pet]
colleague	գործընկեր	[gortsɪ'ŋker]
neighbors	հարևաններ	[areva'ŋer]

4. Human body

body	մարմին	[mar'min]
heart	սիրտ	[sirt]
blood	արյուն	[a'ryn]
brain	ուղեղ	[u'heh]

bone	ոսկոր	[vos'kor]
spine (backbone)	ողնաշար	[vohna'ʃʌr]
rib	կողոսկր	[ko'hoskr]
lungs	թոքեր	[to'ker]
skin	մաշկ	[maʃk]

head	գլուխ	[gluh]
face	երես	[e'res]
nose	քիթ	[kit]
forehead	ճակատ	[tʃa'kat]
cheek	այտ	[ajt]

mouth	բերան	[be'ran]
tongue	լեզու	[le'zu]
tooth	ատամ	[a'tam]
lips	շրթունքներ	[ʃrtuŋk'ner]
chin	կզակ	[kzak]

ear	ականջ	[a'kandʒ]
neck	պարանոց	[para'nots]
eye	աչք	[atʃk]
pupil	բիբ	[bib]
eyebrow	ունք	[uŋk]
eyelash	թարթիչ	[tar'titʃ]
hair	մազեր	[ma'zer]
hairstyle	սանրվածք	[sanr'vatsk]

mustache	բեղեր	[be'her]
beard	մորուք	[mo'ruk]
to have (a beard, etc.)	կրել	[krel]
bald (adj)	ճաղատ	[ʧa'hat]
hand	դաստակ	[das'tak]
arm	թև	[tev]
finger	մատ	[mat]
nail	եղունգ	[e'huŋ]
palm	ափ	[ap]
shoulder	ուս	[us]
leg	ոտք	[votk]
knee	ծունկ	[ʦuŋk]
heel	կրունկ	[kruŋk]
back	մեջք	[medʒk]

5. Clothing. Personal accessories

clothes	հագուստ	[a'gust]
coat (overcoat)	վերարկու	[verar'ku]
fur coat	մուշտակ	[muʃ'tak]
jacket (e.g., leather ~)	բաճկոն	[baʧ'kon]
raincoat (trenchcoat, etc.)	թիկնոց	[tik'nots]
shirt (button shirt)	վերնաշապիկ	[vernaʃʌ'pik]
pants	տաբատ	[ta'bat]
suit jacket	պիջակ	[pi'dʒak]
suit	կոստյում	[kos'tym]
dress (frock)	զգեստ	[zgest]
skirt	շրջազգեստ	[ʃrdʒaz'gest]
T-shirt	մարզաշապիկ	[marzaʃʌ'pik]
bathrobe	խալաթ	[ha'lat]
pajamas	նեգլիզեստ	[ŋdʒaz'gest]
workwear	աշխատանքային հանդգեստ	[aʃhataŋka'jın amaz'gest]
underwear	ներքնազգեստ	[nerknaz'gest]
socks	կիսագուլպա	[kisagul'pa]
bra	կրծկալ	[krtskal]
pantyhose	զուգագուլպա	[zugagul'pa]
stockings (thigh highs)	գուլպաներ	[gulpa'ner]
bathing suit	լողազգեստ	[lohaz'gest]
hat	գլխարկ	[glhark]
footwear	կոշիկ	[ko'ʃik]
boots (cowboy ~)	երկարաճիտ կոշիկներ	[erkara'ʧit koʃik'ner]
heel	կրունկ	[kruŋk]
shoestring	կոշկակապ	[koʃka'kap]

shoe polish	կոշիկի քսուք	[koʃi'ki k'suk]
gloves	ձեռնոցներ	[dzernots'ner]
mittens	ձեռնոց	[dzer'nots]
scarf (muffler)	շարֆ	[ʃʌrf]
glasses (eyeglasses)	ակնոց	[ak'nots]
umbrella	հովանոց	[ova'nots]

tie (necktie)	փողկապ	[poh'kap]
handkerchief	թաշկինակ	[taʃki'nak]
comb	սանր	[sanr]
hairbrush	մազերի խոզանակ	[maze'ri hoza'nak]

buckle	ճարմանդ	[tʃar'mand]
belt	գոտի	[go'ti]
purse	կանացի պայուսակ	[kana'tsi paju'sak]

6. House. Apartment

apartment	բնակարան	[bnaka'ran]
room	սենյակ	[se'ɲak]
bedroom	ննջարան	[ɲdʒa'ran]
dining room	ճաշասենյակ	[tʃaʃʌse'ɲak]

living room	հյուրասենյակ	[jurase'ɲak]
study (home office)	աշխատասենյակ	[aʃhatase'ɲak]
entry room	նախասենյակ	[nahase'ɲak]
bathroom (room with a bath or shower)	լոգարան	[loga'ran]
half bath	զուգարան	[zuga'ran]

vacuum cleaner	փոշեկուլ	[poʃə'kul]
mop	շվաբր	[ʃvabr]
dust cloth	շնորց	[dʒndʒots]
short broom	ավել	[a'vel]
dustpan	աղբական	[ahba'kal]

furniture	կահույք	[ka'ujk]
table	սեղան	[se'han]
chair	աթոռ	[a'tor]
armchair	բազկաթոռ	[bazka'tor]

mirror	հայելի	[aje'li]
carpet	գորգ	[gorg]
fireplace	բուխարի	[buha'ri]
drapes	վարագույր	[vara'gujr]
table lamp	սեղանի լամպ	[seha'ni 'lamp]
chandelier	ջահ	[dʒah]

kitchen	խոհանոց	[hoa'nots]
gas stove (range)	գազօջախ	[gazo'dʒah]

| electric stove | էլեկտրական սալօջախ | [ɛlektra'kan salo'dʒah] |
| microwave oven | միկրոալիքային վառարան | [mikroalika'jın vara'ran] |

refrigerator	սառնարան	[sarna'ran]
freezer	սառնախցիկ	[sarnah'tsik]
dishwasher	աման լվացող մեքենա	[a'man lva'tsoh meke'na]
faucet	ծորակ	[tso'rak]

meat grinder	մսաղաց	[msa'hats]
juicer	հյութաքամիչ	[jutaka'mitʃ]
toaster	տոստեր	[tos'ter]
mixer	հարիչ	[a'ritʃ]

coffee machine	սրճեփ	[srtʃep]
kettle	թեյնիկ	[tej'nik]
teapot	թեյման	[teja'man]

TV set	հեռուստացույց	[ɛrusta'tsujts]
VCR (video recorder)	տեսամագնիտոֆոն	[tesamagnito'fon]
iron (e.g., steam ~)	արդուկ	[ar'duk]
telephone	հեռախոս	[ɛra'hos]

www.ingramcontent.com/pod-product-compliance
Lightning Source LLC
Chambersburg PA
CBHW071505070426
42452CB00041B/2300